T0196604

Pregnancy
and
Parenthood
in a
Foreign Land

My Experience in Thailand with Useful Tips for Mothers Everywhere

REBECCA WONGWIBOONCHAI

BALBOA.
PRESS
A DIVISION OF HAY HOUSE

Balboa Press books may be ordered through booksellers or by contacting:

Balboa Press
A Division of Hay House
1663 Liberty Drive
Bloomington, IN 47403
www.balboapress.com
1 (877) 407-4847

Because of the dynamic nature of the Internet, any web addresses or
links contained in this book may have changed since publication and
may no longer be valid. The views expressed in this work are solely those
of the author and do not necessarily reflect the views of the publisher,
and the publisher hereby disclaims any responsibility for them.

The author of this book does not dispense medical advice or prescribe
the use of any technique as a form of treatment for physical, emotional,
or medical problems without the advice of a physician, either directly
or indirectly. The intent of the author is only to offer information
of a general nature to help you in your quest for emotional and
spiritual well-being. In the event you use any of the information in
this book for yourself, which is your constitutional right, the author
and the publisher assume no responsibility for your actions.

Any people depicted in stock imagery provided by Thinkstock are
models, and such images are being used for illustrative purposes only.
Certain stock imagery © Thinkstock.

Printed in the United States of America.

ISBN: 978-1-5043-2619-3 (sc)
ISBN: 978-1-5043-2620-9 (e)
Library of Congress Control Number: 2015900190

Balboa Press rev. date: 1/2/2015

Dedication

With my deepest love and affection,
I dedicate this book to my two greatest
inspirations: my husband and daughter,
Pramote and Tamina.

Acknowledgements

I would like to express my deepest appreciation to
the many people who have made this book possible:

First, I give thanks to God, my strength and my shield,
for His blessing in giving me an awesome miracle.

To Pramote Wongwiboonchai, my husband
and father of our child, for his tremendous love
and support since the time we first met.

To my father and mother whose teachings – through
their love – will remain with me forever and help me
continue to share my love with my own family.

To one and all who, directly or indirectly, have
lent their helping hand in this book venture.

Thank you!

Contents

Preface

As a young girl, I dreamed of becoming a mom. I loved the idea of being a mother and having my own family to enjoy and look after. Many times I would play "Moms and Dads" with my sisters, friends, and even my teddies! I tended to be the mother, as I liked the control this role entailed.

Many years passed, and I grew up, but I still held the vision of having my own happy family. Then in 2006, I met a wonderful man who was so loving and compassionate. He was the person I knew I wanted to have my dream family with. A few years later, in July 2010, we got married, and this is where living out my family dream began.

To explain how we (I use "we" and "us" throughout the book to refer to me and my husband) came to live in Thailand, I first need to take a step back to explain my career path. Alongside my dream for having a family when I was a child, I also knew that I wanted to be a primary teacher. Every decision made during the course of my education related to my passion for becoming a teacher—from the GCSE and A-Level subjects I chose, the work experience opportunities I took, and the recognized associations I joined. When I completed my A-Levels (these are the advanced level exams in England, which are normally completed at eighteen years of age) and started my BA in primary education course at university, I felt I was definitely on my path to achieving my childhood dream.

During my university years and early years of teaching, I developed an interest in teaching in another country. However, I seemed to hold back on making this move as my idea of a "perfect" family was to find a man, get married, buy a house, own a car, have a secure job, make babies, sign children up to a local school where they would attend for the full stretch of their education, and have complete financial security (such as pensions, making annual tax investments).

When I met my husband, circumstances started to change. My dream of moving to another country to live and work in actually began manifesting itself in the physical world. When looking at places to go on our honeymoon, we had a number of countries in mind. We decided on Thailand because that is where my husband originates from, and he had family members who lived there. Interestingly, Asia, as a continent, never interested me as a place to visit, let alone live and work.

While on our honeymoon I got to meet some of my husband's family members, and we were introduced to a friend who had connections with some of the local international schools. As a result, we got talking about the possibility of me working at a school in Thailand.

Upon returning to England, my husband and I often discussed the possibility of moving to Thailand, including the pros and cons. Then one day when I was doing a job search for international teaching posts in Thailand, I came across a school position for which I was interested in applying. After the necessary applications and interviews I secured that teaching job!

In the summer of 2011, we moved to Thailand to start our new life and, very shortly, our own family. Three and a half months after making the move, I found myself six weeks pregnant!

My Health

I believe the health of a mother is very important in not only creating a healthy baby but also in the nurturing process. Food certainly plays a major part in this, so I want to share a little about my health history and eating habits.

Throughout my life, I have always been slim, bony, tall, and underweight. Since my late teens, I have pretty much stayed the same weight and size. Over the years, I have enjoyed a variety of foods, mostly enjoying my mom's home-cooked meals. Although I occasionally experimented with different recipes, I never considered myself as someone who would cook for her family. This was an area I struggled with on a daily basis, and when I went to university, my diet consisted of mainly fast-food-type meals.

As I grew up, got my teaching qualification, and became a working professional, it became more apparent to me that there were health issues that were affecting my work life and overall social interactions. Some of the health issues included fatigue, lethargy, and irritable bowel syndrome. During this time, I started looking for some "cures" or ways that I could reduce these symptoms. That was when I came across information about food affecting certain conditions in the body. I bought a recipe book that helped explain and treat candida (yeast infection). For a few months, each week I would make batches of delicious wheat-free bread and vegetable soups, slaving away in the kitchen for one day each week. Although this way of eating improved my health a little, it was not how I wanted to spend my life.

I continued researching and experimenting for many years until I eventually came across a raw food diet that consisted of fruits, vegetables, and superfoods, along with other raw condiments. I began following a suggested diet plan that I came across on the Internet that was sold as a plan to give you energy. Like before, I did feel better when following its suggestions, but the amount of ingredients in each meal were many, and the preparation took a lot of time and energy. After following it for only two weeks, I noticed I had lost some weight—weight I could not afford to lose—and I was mentally worn out from all the preparation. Therefore, I moved away from following the diet, occasionally using one or two of the recipes. My search for the "perfect" diet continued.

After much research and looking at book recommendations, I bought the book *80/10/10* by Dr. Douglas Graham. When I received it in the mail, I was eager to read it and find out more about his views on food. After reading a short section, I realized that his diet consisted of mainly fruits and vegetables with little else. I remember my reaction: "I'll never eat meals that are only fruit and of portions that size. I still need to eat meat, grains, and dairy." Little did I know that by the end of reading that book, my opinion would completely change. Everything he wrote made sense to me. I started following his daily suggestions. Now whether it was due to the lack of good quality fruit in England or the environmental pressures I felt, I was unable to commit to this change in lifestyle, although I did increase my overall intake of fruits and vegetables. There was noticeable improvement to my health when I did so. Then we moved to Thailand!

When we got to Thailand and started a family, I decided that I needed to be pickier with my food and drink choices. I have never been a big alcohol drinker— my weakness was with Pepsi. I found myself drinking less Pepsi, and, being in a tropical climate, I favored drinking young coconut water where available. As a result, not drinking Pepsi did not cause much of an upset. The main drinks I had were water, young coconut water, shop-bought juices, and flavored milk.

By the time I became pregnant, I was eating and drinking what is considered to be a "healthy," balanced diet according to many health enthusiasts, and I enjoyed the food I was eating.

About This Book

When I got the idea to write this book, I felt this would be my opportunity to share my journey with readers and that they would value a different perspective on pregnancy and parenthood, especially if some are expats experiencing a different country, culture, and health-care system. Through sharing my experiences while living abroad and becoming a mother, readers will be provided with relatable anecdotes and a number of useful tips, which can be translated to most countries.

Each chapter has two main sections. The first section is "A Real-life Experience," which details the events of my experiences while pregnant, going through labor, and experiencing early motherhood. The second section is titled "The Facts," which provides useful information (along with general information and customs more specific to Thailand) and helpful tips for each stage.

CHAPTER 1

Pregnancy

A Real-life Experience

Pregnancy: First Trimester

This chapter in my life began in August 2011, when my husband and I had recently moved to Thailand for a change in job opportunities and the chance to experience life in a different country and culture. We had not been in Thailand long before we decided that it would be a suitable time to start a family of our own.

With our intention of me becoming pregnant, I became more conscious of what I ate and drank. Because I was in a new country where the way of life was very different from what I was used to and my exposure to a range of new foods—many of which I had never even heard of before—was vast, I felt there was a big learning curve taking place.

A big part of Thai culture is to eat out, whether in a

restaurant or on the roadside. Kitchens are very minimal and do not really cater to family cooking. My husband and I often ate out or bought something precooked to eat later. With the goal of becoming pregnant, my intake of fizzy drinks and prawns was reduced to virtually zero, as I was aware of the possible health risks of consuming these items. My new work colleagues often asked me about when I was planning on getting pregnant and why I was not eating and drinking certain items. As I did not know them very well, I was able to pass their comments off by vaguely replying, "I've never really liked it much anyway."

One food-related issue that seemed to crop up in most discussions around food was the use of monosodium glutamate (MSG). I had only ever read about this substance in health-related books, but it had never caused me great concern or been something I came across when cooking in England. However, I soon realized that it is prevalent in many Thai foods, and I tried to avoid it where possible.

During the month leading up to the realization that I was pregnant, I felt that I was not quite myself, as my stomach felt a bit uncomfortable every now and then, and my urine started to have a different odor. Throughout my first trimester, I noticed changes in my body: I found myself having less energy and getting tired quickly, and my stomach was stretching ever so slightly. Because it had never been big, it was a new feeling for me, and it felt a little bit painful. It was already uncomfortable to sleep on my front or back, so I started sleeping on my side during the night. Small, protruding moles started to appear on my neck and shoulder area.

My abdominal area itched occasionally, and at one time, I had a few red spots in that area. I was not having regular bowel movements; I needed to go about every two days. I also found myself reacting strangely to the smells of certain foods. For example, the school canteen was somewhere I did not want to hang around in for very long, as I could not stand the overpowering smell of rice.

One morning, I noticed some blood, so I ruled out being pregnant, thinking it was the beginning of my monthly period. Later on that day, I had no more blood, so I asked my husband to get a pregnancy test. That evening, I took the test, and within three minutes, my suspicions were confirmed—I was pregnant! We were both overjoyed with the test result, but of course, we wanted it confirmed by a doctor.

The following day, after having spent pretty much a whole day on a coach doing a visa run to Cambodia, I went to hospital to get myself checked by a doctor. This initial doctor's appointment was made by a relative, as we were unsure what the procedure was in Thailand. The health care system is very different than that of England, the National Health Service (NHS). It was actually quite simple, as all we needed to do was choose a hospital, register with the hospital using my passport details, and then go to the necessary department.

I was assigned to a female doctor who could speak at a good level of English, and my husband could translate information where necessary. The doctor gave me a transvaginal ultrasound, which involved a probe, called a transducer, placed in the vagina. The probe sends out sound waves, creating a picture on a computer. The procedure confirmed that I was definitely pregnant. The doctor also carried out a smear test to check that my cervix was in a healthy state for pregnancy. There was some cell abnormality, so I was given a pessary that I was to insert for the following three nights. From the scan, she also pointed out that there was a blood clot, so I needed to take extra care—no speed boat rides for me!

As soon as the doctor confirmed my pregnancy, I immediately asked questions about what foods I could eat while pregnant, especially since I was in a foreign country and had a range of unfamiliar foods available to me. The doctor informed me that I could eat all foods. However, because of my extensive research about food and pregnancy, there were foods that I still avoided, such as seafood, cold meats, and certain cheeses. I was given many different opinions about what tropical fruits were safe to consume and the effects they could have on my body and my unborn child. I decided to eat those that were ripe and that my body responded well to. I returned to the same doctor for a ten-week checkup but then decided that the travelling distance was too far, especially with the traffic in Bangkok, so we looked for a closer facility.

My first trimester passed, and my pregnancy was going well. The blood clot that showed up in my initial scan was gone, and my fetus was developing as expected.

Pregnancy: Second Trimester

During this trimester, I felt I got my energy back and was able to accomplish more than in the previous term. I continued working but was aware of my need to take care of myself and not lift heavy objects. It was at about twelve weeks that I felt my baby move.

My husband and I researched hospitals and had a look around some. We finally settled on an international hospital, as its staff members were friendly and welcoming. The hospital staff showed us around the labor and aftercare rooms, and the package was what we wanted. Due to changing hospitals, we needed to arrange for the blood test results and other paperwork to be transferred, which was easily done by contacting the doctor via e-mail and having the information sent to my home.

My first checkup at our newly chosen hospital involved the regular weight check, being asked my height, and having my temperature and blood pressure checked. I was also required to give a urine sample during most visits. Every time after measuring my temperature, the staff would reassure me that I did not have a fever. I found this amusing.

Not being sure of the protocol for checkups, we were unsure of what to expect. On our first visit to the new hospital, I was in a private room with my husband and parents, who were on holiday from England, with me lying ready on a bed and a big screen in front of us. As I was getting into position for the ultrasound, a small bump, my baby, popped up in my tummy and stayed there for a bit. We were very excited. When the doctor came in, he began scanning the area. To our amazement and due to the modern technology, we could see a very lifelike image of our baby on the screen. The doctor took many measurements and photos as he progressed with the scan to check our baby's development. All was going great. After the scan, we were given a photo booklet and CD with images from the scan—a lovely gift to treasure.

At our nineteen-week checkup, my husband needed to have a blood test. The blood test results showed that he was RhD-positive. Due to me being RhD-negative, I found out that I would need to have two injections, called anti-D immunoglobin, that prevent the baby from any harm from rhesus incompatibility. I would be given the first of these at twenty-eight weeks and the second shot within seventy-two hours of giving birth.

At this point, I was getting big and gaining weight steadily. I had convinced many people that I was having a boy because, in the early stages, I was convinced of this myself as my three sisters all had girls first so I thought it'd be a boy given the ratio. It wasn't until we went for our nineteen-week checkup that it was confirmed I was having a girl, just like my sisters!

At following checkups, we had 4-D ultrasounds, as we were very impressed with the first and wanted to see our darling baby. However, the scans were not very clear because she had grown so much and was camera shy!

As mentioned previously, my second trimester gave me some energy back as I continued to enjoy my pregnancy and the excitement it created between me and my husband. My interest in food returned, but I did not experience any cravings.

Pregnancy: Third Trimester

During this trimester, I noticed a change again in my energy level because my bump was getting bigger and heavier to carry around. I walked around at an even slower pace and minimized walking up and down stairs, which I needed to do at work. Standing up and sitting down required more effort and care, particularly if it was a low chair, as I could not bend forward as much as I normally could to propel myself from a seated position. I worked out ways of getting myself up—for example, by holding on to my knees or with the help of my husband.

Getting up from a lying position was also becoming more of a challenge. At this point in pregnancy, I could sleep only on my sides and found sleeping on my left side more comfortable. Shifting around while sleeping became increasingly difficult, and I needed to take care, as I could not lie on my back or front. When getting up in the morning, I needed to move my body to the side of the bed, hang my legs over the edge, and push myself up with my arms.

In addition to this challenge, I also regularly experienced tingling in my legs due to the circulation being cut off. To relieve this, I needed to move my legs around as much as possible to get the blood flowing again.

After a day's work, I noticed that sometimes my ankles were swollen; however, this decreased with rest. I also tended to get a pain in my right side, especially in the late afternoon/evening when walking around. I just let my body rest when this happened.

At our twenty-eight-week checkup, the doctor informed us that our baby's head was down in the pelvic area under the belly button, which I was relieved to hear. Her head stayed down for the remainder of the pregnancy, and I experienced nerve pain in the trunks of my thighs, possibly from where her head was putting pressure.

My baby became very lively during this final trimester. I mostly felt her movements when my body was at rest, usually at bedtime. My husband and I would often talk and sing to her, placing our hands on my bump and gently rubbing. We noticed on occasion that there was sometimes a clicking sound, like fingernails tapping together. This did cause us some concern, so we researched and found that this is quite common, although no one is clear about what it is. The most popular idea is that the baby's bones are clicking as it moves. I continued to monitor the regularity of the clicking, but it was very sporadic, so I did not worry about it. At our thirty-three-week checkup, I had an HIV test.

I found myself feeling an increase in hunger but ensured that I continued eating regular meals and healthy snacks. I purchased a juicer and started making my own vegetable juices to ensure that I consumed a variety of vital minerals and vitamins at recommended levels. I noticed quite early on in my pregnancy that my baby liked coconut water, as there was always some movement after I drank it.

At 35 weeks of pregnancy, I experienced moments of pain in my pelvic area, particularly on my left side. This tended to include pains in the top of my left thigh and occasionally in the buttocks, where the sciatic nerve is located. I did wonder if this was a symptom of Braxton-Hicks contractions, but I was unsure as my stomach also tensed up irregularly. I found that taking a warm shower temporarily eased the discomfort.

I stopped working at 36 weeks because the school summer holiday began. We did very little during this time, as it took me a lot of effort to move around. When we did go out for a day, I enjoyed the following day relaxing at home to revitalize myself.

During this trimester, I researched and prepared a birthing plan, which I shared with my doctor (see Appendix A for a copy of my birthing plan). I used Google Translate so that it was also in Thai. Although I had written and shared my birthing plan, I knew the events would not necessarily happen as planned in reality, but it helped communicate my wishes to those involved with the labor and aftercare of my baby.

The hospital we went to offered an antenatal class that we chose to take advantage of. At the class, they explained the birthing process, using videos to demonstrate how the baby is born. Breathing techniques were demonstrated, and then I was given an opportunity to practice my breathing with a nurse's coaching. The class was conducted in Thai, so my husband translated as much as he could, although there was quite a lot of technical language that he did not know. It was a worthwhile experience; plus we were given a few "freebies" from company brands.

The following are the standard charges (2012) for every checkup:

Laboratory investigation (urine sample) = 126 baht
NSG charge (midwifery) = 330 baht
Packed medical charge: OPD charge = 150 baht
First outpatient care = 400 baht
Total = 1,006 baht

Note also that Thai hospitals can charge Thai prices and foreigner prices. It is worth asking about this to see if they will give you the Thai price, especially if you are living in the country.

Pregnancy: The Facts

Pregnancy Symptoms

I am guessing that you are reading this book because you already know that you are pregnant. What were your symptoms?

Here is a list of the top ten symptoms according to www.babycentre.co.uk:

1. Prickling, tingling nipples
2. Spotting and cramping
3. Feeling sick
4. Tender, swollen breasts
5. Feeling tired
6. Needing to urinate frequently
7. Darker nipples
8. Food cravings and an altered sense of smell
9. A missed period
10. The proof: a positive home pregnancy test

(The Top 10 Signs of Pregnancy, BabyCentre, 2013).

Checkups

You can schedule your checkups for times that best suits you, including the day, time, and how often (although there are certain weeks when your doctor will encourage you to go so they can monitor particular stages in fetal development). Checkups tend to include the following procedures:

- Weight check
- Height check
- Blood pressure check
- Temperature check
- Urine check
- A discussion with the doctor about how the pregnancy is progressing and a chance to ask any questions
- An ultrasound

It is important for the hospital to know the blood types of the expectant mother and father due to possible blood complications during the birth as well as to check if there is a chance of conflicting blood types between mother and baby. Therefore, hospitals carry out routine blood tests for both parents-to-be. If the mother-to-be tests rhesus positive, then all is okay, and no further action needs to be taken. However, if mother-to-be tests *rhesus negative* and the father-to-be is *positive*, then she will require an *anti-D injection* later on in the pregnancy and one following the birth of her child. This is due to the possibility of the mother's blood and the baby's blood being incompatible and triggering an immune response, which causes the body to develop antibodies that fight against the baby's blood as though it were a foreign invader. This process is called sensitization (Rhesus Negative and the Anti-D Injection, Mumsnet By Parents for Parents, 2013).

Hospitals

When you are in Thailand or most other countries that require you to pay for your medical expenses, you have many choices to make when you find yourself pregnant. The following is a list of options you might like to consider when making your choices:

- Location of the hospital: You will be making regular visits prior to the birth and also if you continue with the hospital's aftercare (vaccinations and general checkups).
- Cost of birthing package and what it includes: There are a number of hospitals to choose from, particularly in Bangkok, which range from government to international hospitals, each catering to different needs and wishes.
- Type of birth: natural birth, Caesarean birth, water birth, or home birth. Thailand does not allow home births, and there is currently only one known hospital that will provide a water birth (Samitivej Hospital, Srinakarin, Bangkok).
- Doctor: You have the choice about whether you want a male or female doctor, and you can meet him or her to decide whether you want that

doctor to deliver your baby. Also, check whether the doctor is willing to adhere as closely as possible to your birthing plan. (See Appendix B for a comprehensive list of 'Things you might want to ask your doctor about.")

- Language: Some hospitals may offer support to non-native speakers. If you choose an international hospital, then the doctor will probably speak a sufficient amount of English; however, some of your questions or concerns might be misunderstood.

- Afterbirth care: It is important to inquire about the hospitals policy for access to your baby after he or she is born. Some hospitals keep all newborns in a separate area from the mother (sometimes even on a different floor level) and therefore require the mother to visit. However, other hospitals keep mother and baby in the same zone so the baby can be brought into the room at any time or the mother can just step outside her room.

- One last point to consider, though it may not be as important, is whether the hospital conducts 4-D ultrasound scans.

<u>Note:</u> In hospitals, you do not get the bill until you are at the checkout.

Food

While you are pregnant, it is important to eat a healthy diet. It is also important to keep in mind that just because you are pregnant, you are not eating for two! During the first trimester, you might find that you go no longer have a taste for certain foods; however, it is important to ensure that what you do eat is nutritious for you and your fetal development.

Fruits and vegetables (including leafy greens) are essentials when pregnant, as they provide vitamins and minerals, as well as fiber, which can help with digestion. It is best to eat them fresh because the nutrient quality is better, but frozen, canned, or dried is also good. A way to ensure you eat a suitable amount of vegetables is to make green juices. These can be by either extracting the juice from vegetables using a juicer or pulverizing them in a blender. The bonus of using a blender is that you still eat the fiber of the vegetables. By drinking freshly made juices, your body is instantly provided with numerous vitamins and minerals since the juicing process breaks the fibers down, so they are easily assimilated by the body. Due to possible detoxing when making changes to your diet, it is suggested that any major changes be made gradually so that there is less chance for toxins to cross the barrier to the fetus.

Starchy foods, such as rice, pasta, noodles, sweet potatoes, and oats, are considered a good source of carbohydrates since these foods are also an important source of vitamins and fiber. However, eat brown rice and wholemeal varieties of pasta as these are a healthier option to than the white, processed varieties (Rhesus Negative and the Anti-D Injection, NHS, 2013).

During your pregnancy, you might be concerned about whether you are consuming enough protein. There are the well-known sources of protein, such as meat (avoid liver), fish, poultry, eggs, beans, pulses, and nuts; however, another rich source of protein can be provided by consuming leafy greens. They are a very healthy and clean way of receiving a number of beneficial vitamins and minerals, especially if they are organic. If you are at all concerned about how changing from an animal-based diet to one that is more plant-based might affect tissue growth, consider looking at the animal kingdom and identifying animals that eat a plant-based diet. There are rabbits (okay, so that is a small mammal), monkeys, gorillas, giraffes, and even elephants! All these animals grow by eating a plant-based diet. To find out more about the appropriate amount of protein humans need to consume, it is suggested that you read *The 80/10/10 Diet* by Dr. Douglas N. Graham.

If you are consuming animal products, ensure that they come from a reliable source and are cooked thoroughly. It is advisable to avoid eating cold meats, unpasteurized dairy products (such as milk and certain cheeses), and to "eat no more than two portions of oily fish a week…because pollutants found in oily fish may affect the development of a baby in the womb" (Fish and Shellfish, NHS, 2013).

The following table provides a list of some useful phrases when eating out in Thailand.

English	Thai Pronunciation
No MSG (monosodium glutamate)	Mai sai pong churot
Don't use so much oil.	Chai naammun noi-noi
No sugar	Mai sai naam-dtaan
Lean meat	Neua maid tit mun
Less rice	Kao noi-noi
Not spicy	Mai pet
No chili	Mai sai prik

(Bingo 2013, pp. 61)

Position of Baby

By thirty-two weeks, in most cases, the baby's head is down in the pelvis, with his or her bottom under your diaphragm. If the baby is not in this position yet, do not worry; chances are that he or she will turn before he or she is ready to make an appearance. However, if the baby is head up (also known as "breech") close to the due date, it is worth discussing options with your doctor. To encourage your baby to turn, there are a variety of traditional methods. The one I used was getting on all fours with my head resting down on my arms and visualizing my baby turning (Johnson's Mother & Baby).

CHAPTER 2

Labor and Birth

A Real-life Experience

It was 21:30 on Saturday night. We had just returned from having dinner at the hotel adjacent to our condo. My stomach seemed to keep tensing more than usual throughout the day. I did not feel unusually uncomfortable, but to be on the safe side, we decided to get me checked out at the hospital.

When we arrived at the hospital, I was taken to the labor room in a wheelchair, which seemed strange because I was able to walk (although I did enjoy the pampering). Initially, the medical staff made my husband wait outside the labor department, not realizing he was my husband. However, when I told them who he was—and they had overcome their surprise and embarrassment—they called him in to be with me.

I was in a room for the staff to check my cervix and feel my stomach. They soon told me that I was three centimeters dilated and would be staying in the hospital from now on. Wow! What we had been waiting for over the last nine months was actually starting to happen! After that, the nurse surprised me by shaving my pubic region and then giving me an enema. Not knowing what an enema was, I felt unprepared and embarrassed for having to rush as fast as I could to the toilet and expel everything in my bowels. I was soon empty, given a wash bag, and proceeded to clean myself up in preparation for the waiting game. In the meantime, my husband returned home to get the baby bag and, more importantly, the camera.

From this point on, the nurses wanted me to sleep and get rest. They hooked me up to a heart monitor that fit around my stomach, but it was uncomfortable and loud. It was pretty much impossible to get any sleep. First, I was really excited now that the moment for my baby to enter into the world had nearly arrived; second, the machines were loud and uncomfortable; and third, I had nurses continuously coming in the room to check on me and take my blood pressure and temperature.

After a while of lying down and not sleeping, the nurses allowed me to get out of bed and walk around the room. I did a number of laps, slowly and gently, enjoying the last moments of my pregnancy. I grew thirstier and thirstier and was surprised to be told by the nurse that I was not allowed any food or drink. I did not expect this, but I followed their rules, as I did not know what to expect. I thought that they knew best and had their reasons for this rule. However, in hindsight and for future reference, it is okay to drink water.

Morning came, and the nurse wanted to connect me to a drip of what I think was oxytocin. Having done my research about this labor-inducing drug, I refused. She consulted with the doctor, who said I did not have to have it at that time. Later on, my regular doctor came to check my cervix and was surprised to find that it was not dilated as much as was thought the night before. So the waiting and thirst continued, along with the hourly temperature and blood pressure checks.

Eventually, at about two o'clock in the afternoon, my water broke. Soaking in bed was a strange experience. From that point on, after the bed sheets were changed, I lay in wait. This time, I was connected to the drip and not given the opportunity to decline. The nurses started getting the stirrups ready, but I told them that I did not want them and would like to be kneeling in an upright position while giving birth. Again, after looking at me strangely and asking permission from the doctor, they took them away.

While I was lying there on my own (my husband had gone out for a moment), one of the nurses came in wanting to take some blood. I did not, and still do not, fully understand why she did this. From what I did understand, it was apparently a blood donation for the Red Cross, although she took only a small syringe, hardly enough for much use. I continued lying in bed with ever-growing excitement.

At about half past three that afternoon, things really started to set in motion. My contractions were getting stronger, and I was feeling the urge to push. In came all the nurses, and the birth process began. Every so often when I could feel a contraction, everyone in the room would encourage me to breath and push. It sounded quite amusing, but at the same time, I was reciting The Lord's Prayer in my head to help me focus and to give thanks for the miracle about to appear. For each contraction, there was a nurse standing over me, assisting my pushing by pushing just below my ribcage. I did not think there was anything wrong with it at the time, but I later found out that this practice can be dangerous and is actually against the law in some countries. Anyway, this continued for just over an hour. I was lying on my back the whole time with my husband dabbing my forehead with cold flannels that quickly turned hot from all my sweat.

After I pushed for over an hour, the doctor decided that I needed some help because where my baby's head was pushing on my pelvic bone was not good for either of us. Out came the stirrups, and I was given a catheter to remove any remaining liquid in my bladder. Then came the vacuum, which would suck my baby out. Shortly after this process, at ten minutes past five in the early evening, my baby girl was born. She was passed to me, still connected via the umbilical cord, and I put her on my breast straight away. What a miracle! My husband and I both agreed on her name straightaway: Tamina.

After holding her for about five minutes and having some first photos snapped, she was taken to be weighed, cleaned, and to have all the other medical procedures for newborns done. My husband stayed with our baby while I was taken care of. My baby's placenta was removed, and I was given a few stitches where I naturally split during the birthing process.

After being sewn back together, cleaned up, and given

my second rhesus negative injection, I was left alone with instructions to rest. However, I was far too excited to do that! Everything that had just happened kept playing over in my mind, and I was very much looking forward to seeing my baby again. It was not until about eight o'clock, when my husband and I were settled in our room, that I got to be with my baby again.

The Facts

Labor Signs

There are a number of pre-labor signs, but the following are just some of the most obvious and common ones taken from www.babycentre.co.uk:

- "Painful contractions that occur at regular, increasingly shorter intervals and become longer and stronger in intensity.
- Broken water. Your membranes may rupture with a gush or a trickle of amniotic fluid.
- A brownish or blood-tinged mucus discharge (bloody show). If you pass the mucus plug that blocks the cervix, labor could be imminent, or it could be several days away. It's a sign that things are moving along" (Signs of Labour, BabyCentre, 2013).
- When your water breaks, it is a good idea to make your way to the hospital if you have not done so already, especially if you live in a place with a lot of traffic, such as Bangkok.

- The mucus plug should not consist of a lot of blood. If you suspect anything wrong with the discharge, seek medical advice immediately.

Thai Hospital Routines

When you are admitted to hospital, you will be required to sign a contract that gives your agreement to allow the hospital to perform necessary procedures while under their care.

If you want to record the birth or take pictures, then it is advised you check with the doctor prior to giving birth. It is against the policy of some hospitals to take video of births for legal reasons.

Birthing plans are useful to have, especially if there is a language barrier and you wish to have your "ideal labor" communicated to your doctor. It is suggested that you share this with your doctor at a suitable checkup close to the due date. (See Appendix A for an example of a birthing plan.) Some useful terminology for this is as follows:

- Epidural: This is an injection in the lower back that numbs the nerves and stops you from feeling pain (Epidural Anesthesia, NHS, 2013).
- Amniotomy: This is an artificial rupture of the membranes, causing your water to break.
- Episiotomy: Doctors may make small cuts in your cervix to aid in the birth of your child and stop you from tearing naturally.

In Thai hospitals, traditional delivery, in which the woman lies on a hospital bed with leg rests, is favored. It can be challenging to request an alternative position, such as lying on your left side with your right leg raised or kneeling up, even though these are suggested as better positions to aid in a smoother delivery (Johnson's Mother & Baby).

As soon as your baby is born, he or she will be taken away to be cleaned and a number of tests will be conducted, such as listening to the heart and lungs, feeling the abdomen, checking movement in the hips and limbs, as well as a spine check to make sure all the vertebrae are in place. It is important to note that your baby will usually be given a Vitamin K injection, and silver nitrates or antibiotic eye ointment will likely be used to clean his eyes (Beier, 2013). To find more information on these procedures, check out the "Giving Birth Naturally" Web site at http://www.givingbirthnaturally.com/newborn-baby-care.html.

CHAPTER 3

First Days of Motherhood

A Real-life Experience

Wow! I was now a mother. We were overjoyed to have our little baby girl with us in the world. It felt great and was such a miracle to be holding my baby in my arms after carrying her for thirty-eight weeks.

After feeding Tamina and enjoying our first family time together, she was taken to an enclosed area so that we could all get some rest.

She was brought to us again about three hours later for a feeding. We loved having her with us, and it felt strange each time they took her away. Feeding time continued every three hours.

It was always my intention to breastfeed; I did not want my baby to have any formula. My breasts were producing milk from the moment my baby was born; however, there was not very much. Due to this small supply and the fact that my baby was a bit jaundiced, the nurses wanted to give her formula to ensure that she did not become dehydrated. After consulting with my husband, I let him feed her some formula and, thankfully, she was not that interested and definitely preferred my breast.

In the morning, we were asked where we wanted Tamina to have her Bacillus Calmette–Guérin (BCG) vaccination against tuberculosis: her arm or her bottom. Surprised at her having this vaccination at birth, we chose her arm as that is where we had it when we were teenagers.

The first day after her birth included a breast massage, as my breasts were hard and big from the milk coming through, a heated lamp shining on my vagina for fifteen minutes, a lot of cuddles with the baby and my husband, having my temperature and blood pressure checked, and getting some rest. Each time I had a checkup, I was asked if I had a bowel movement. Due to having had an enema and not eating or drinking for twenty-four hours, I had not.

Since giving birth the previous day, I was hooked up to a drip that I think was meant to help my sugar levels, but the doctors and nurses were not very clear about what it was and why it was necessary. Thankfully, some of my blood kept going up the tube rather than the liquid going into my body, so they eventually abandoned it and I was free to move around. I was also given some tablets that I was told to take to avoid infection as well as painkillers.

While at the hospital, we did not need to change Tamina's diaper except when they gave us a lesson on how to give your baby a bath and put on a cloth diaper.

This was a useful session, but I relied on my husband to do the practical task and remember the steps since I was feeling tired and quite exhausted. On one occasion when Tamina was brought to us, we noticed that her nails had been cut. This made me wonder what else they did with our daughter while she was not with us, but I decided that I needed to trust the nurses and get rest while I could. After all, we would soon have her at home with just us and no nurses.

Going to the toilet after giving birth was okay, and the nurses helped me with walking to the bathroom and cleaning myself after. One time when I went to the toilet, something big fell out of my vagina. Unsure of what it was and a bit worried, I asked my husband to call for a nurse. To my relief, nothing was wrong. It was just more of the placenta coming out. Over the next few days, smaller pieces kept coming out. I continued bleeding for about a week after giving birth. I had prepared myself for this with long, thick sanitary pads.

Tuesday afternoon came, and it was time for us to get ready to return home now as a family of three. Before taking our baby, we had to pay for the medical care and give the receipt to the baby unit before leaving. We had brought a car seat (Maxi Cosi) and blankets. However, we did not realize that the blankets needed to be washed before use. Thankfully the hospital provided clothing and a blanket for going home. Upon departure, we were given a CD that contained photos of the hospital, us at the birthing class, the birth of Tamina, and Tamina's first photo shoot, where she was dressed in a frilly outfit.

At this time, we were unable to organize Tamina's

birth certificate as we needed to have our passports for identification. On our following visit to the hospital, we presented our identification, and the birth certificate was produced and translated into English for us at a small cost.

We were ready to venture out on our own as new parents with our daughter. When we arrived home, we got organized with washing all the baby items, getting formula and bottles at the ready (although we ended up not using them), changing Tamina's diaper, making a mess of changing her diaper, and getting ready for bed.

Bedtime came. I was even more exhausted! Tamina wanted feeding often, so I had only broken sleep. My husband was also feeling tired. This felt like the most challenging night of my life thus far. I reassured myself by saying that it would not always be like this. Well, over the next week or so, I gradually caught up with my lost sleep and started to feel "human" again. Tamina fed regularly about every one to two hours. Her jaundice was improving, and when we went for a checkup on her first Friday in the world, the doctor was happy with her progress.

I, on the other hand, had developed a rash that spread all over my body. It started to appear on the Thursday after Tamina's birth. I talked to my mom on Skype about it, and she questioned the medication I had been given. One of the tablets was amoxicillin. My mum informed me that she was unable to take penicillin, and my nana could not have either of the drugs. That answered my concerns. All the same, when we took Tamina in for her Friday checkup, we asked the doctor about my rash. He referred me to the skin specialist in the hospital, so off we went.

After an examination, the skin specialist concluded that there was a chance of it being rubella. However, I was not convinced since I did not have symptoms of rubella apart from a rash that did not itch. She told me not to breastfeed, take some medication, and wear a face mask. I wore the face mask until got home; I decided not to take the medication, and my husband tried giving Tamina formula while I pumped milk that was to be thrown away because if I did have some virus I didn't want her catching it through my milk. This lasted until that evening, when I spoke to my mom again and decided that the skin doctor's suggestion was not appropriate and went back to breast-feeding.

The following morning my rash had lessened, so I was convinced it was a reaction to the medication I had been given after giving birth.

The first few days of motherhood continued by taking each moment at a time, catching up on sleep when we could, eating when we needed food, and caring for Tamina's needs.

The Facts

Vaccinations

There is a lot of controversy surrounding whether vaccinations are important, necessary, and safe. You have a responsibility and a certain level of choice about whether your child is to have them and which ones. There are many Web sites and books that explain different vaccinations, and it is worth doing some research on them.

Keep a record of any vaccinations given, as your child might need them later on in life as proof that he or she has received them; otherwise, he or she might be given another vaccine unnecessarily. Some birthing packages include the first-year vaccinations, and if you choose this package, then you will find it works out cheaper than paying for each vaccination individually.

The vaccines given will vary depending on the country you live in. In Thailand, the first year's program of immunization is as follows:

New born = BCG Vaccine (against tuberculosis) and Hepatitis B vaccine, first dose

One month = Hepatitis B vaccine, second dose

Two months = DPT vaccine (diphtheria + tetanus toxoids combined with pertussis vaccine); OPV (oral polio vaccine), first dose; and Hib (Haemophilus influenzae type b vaccine against childhood meningitis and pneumonia), first dose★

Four months = DPT + OPV, second dose and Hib, second dose

Six months = DPT + OPV, third dose and Hib, third dose

Nine months = MMR vaccine (measles, mumps, and rubella vaccine), first dose

Twelve months = Encephalitis vaccine x 2 (one to two weeks apart) and after one year, varicella vaccine

★Up to the judgment of physicians and parents; however, if you choose for your child not to have the vaccine, you must go to a local doctor since the hospitals only give the vaccine as a combination, so it cannot be separated.

Jaundice

Jaundice is a condition that is common in newborns and refers to the yellowing of the skin and whites of the eyes. It is caused by excess bilirubin in the blood, which is produced by the normal breakdown of red blood cells (Jaundice in Newborns, Kids Health, 2014).

It is important for a jaundiced baby to be hydrated. Also, a daily dose of sunshine will help. If natural sunlight is not available, your doctor might suggest phototherapy. Get your baby checked regularly by a doctor. Mild cases of jaundice should clear up within one to two weeks of your baby's life since the liver should have developed enough to get rid of excess bilirubin.

Baby Hernia

After you have gotten over the initial enjoyment of giving birth and cuddling up to your baby, you might notice his belly button protruding. Do not be alarmed! This is likely a baby umbilical hernia (a lump under the skin in the stomach or groin area). Yes, babies can have hernias. Although it does not look very attractive and can be perceived as painful, your baby is fine. A baby hernia happens because the baby's muscles have not fully developed yet. With time, the hernia will recede (Hernias, BabyCentre, 2013).

Mongolian Blue spot

In some cases, babies can have a blue-gray blemish on their lower back or buttocks region, closely resembling a bruise. This is known as a Mongolian blue spot. It is like a birthmark that causes no pain and should disappear by the time your child reaches three to five years old or definitely by puberty (Mongolian Spot, Wikipedia, 2008).

Breast-feeding

Breast-feeding creates an emotional bond between mother and baby, making it an important action to do soon after birth, if not immediately. Ensure that if you choose to breast-feed, your doctor knows your wishes (this is your choice!). Although your breasts might not be producing milk yet, the sucking action and closeness will help release your milk. When the milk is on its way, your breasts will swell and harden. This can be uncomfortable initially, but by placing a warm, wet cloth on them and lightly massaging the area, they will relax and not be so painful. It is also important to note here the wonders of nature: your body will produce what is necessary for your baby. Your baby will not necessarily need large amounts of milk soon after birth, but he or she will need your love and cuddles.

If there happens to be a time when you need to stop giving your baby breast milk for medical reasons (such as you need to take a course of medicine that will not be suitable for your baby) but wish to continue giving it after any medical issues have cleared up, then it is important to continue pumping milk from your breasts and discarding it. Once you stop breast-feeding, your milk soon dries up, and, although it can be possible to start again, this is not always certain or an easy process.

CHAPTER 4

Motherhood: Breast-feeding, Travelling, and Working

A Real-life Experience

Breast-feeding

I prepared myself for breast-feeding, not only physically but mentally as well. I was determined to provide my baby with my milk even while I worked, so I researched breast pumps and how to express milk efficiently in a working lifestyle. My research led me to buying an electric pump that expresses from both breasts simultaneously. I also watched examples of ways to wash, store, and sterilize the equipment. Yes, this was the pump for me! A Medela Freestyle. I ordered it online to be delivered to my parent's house in England with a plan for them to bring it out when they were to visit about a month after Tamina's birth. In the meantime and for small milk expresses, I purchased a Pigeon Hand Pump that got the job done effectively.

I fed on demand, and I always had enough milk. Feeding drained my energy, so I needed to ensure that I consumed enough healthy food to keep my levels up. It was also recommended to drink a cup of room-temperature water before and after feeding to reduce the chances of dehydration. When we were out and about and Tamina needed feeding or her diaper changed, we often went to a baby room in one of the big shopping malls. If there was not one available, we just did the best we could.

Travelling

A couple of months after Tamina was born, we decided to go on a holiday for a few days to a place a couple of hours out of Bangkok. We travelled there in a public minivan, using our Maxi Cosi car seat. Although there were no appropriate seat belts to secure the car seat in place, it was better she was in one than not.

We used the car seat for travelling in taxis around Bangkok until she got too big and heavy for it. Then we started taking her out in the Baby Bjorn Carrier, carrying her the whole time we were out. The bonus of this was that I was able to feed her discretely while walking around.

For Tamina's first Christmas, we decided to fly home to England. We booked two adult seats located at the front end of a section in the plane that had a cot table. It was the night of our departure, and we had everything ready. We got our bags checked in. Then we went through the departure gate. At the passport security desk, we were asked to go to another security section where we were questioned about Tamina. They wanted to see her birth certificate, as it was her first time flying. Not knowing that this was necessary for first-time flyers, we did not have it with us. I was getting a bit flustered thinking we would have to go home and get it. Thankfully, they asked us the details of where and when she was born, did their necessary checks, and let us continue with our journey.

Once on the plane, I was given a baby seat belt for takeoff and landing that connected into mine. At these times, I encouraged Tamina to feed, as the sucking would help with the changes in cabin pressure. I also sang to her. After takeoff, we were given a cot but soon found out that Tamina did not fit in the cot basket. Instead, we borrowed the car seat style for her, which she did not like going in much, but we were able to put her in it for a short while after she had fallen asleep. Tamina travelled well in the plane with lots of cuddles and feeding on demand.

Travelling by car in England was much easier than getting taxis in Thailand, as we had our own car and used the car seat. We also had a buggy to push her in around the shops rather than carrying her. Tamina enjoyed her new experiences.

Working

I had ninety days maternity leave from work. It had been our intention, even before getting pregnant, that when we were to have children, one of us would be the stay-at-home parent. Due to my work commitment, this meant my husband was the one for the job. The week before I returned to work, we started introducing Tamina to a bottle for feeding. It was not until I was back at work, and so unavailable for feeding her, that she started properly having feeds from it. When I returned home, though, she wanted to have long feeds with me.

At work, I found a semi-private and quiet place where I could express my milk. I only pumped once during the day, at lunchtimes, for about twenty minutes. I stored my milk in the fridge, which I then collected before going home, putting it in a cool bag for travel. After pumping, I rinsed the necessary pump parts and put them in a sealed plastic bag, ready to take home, wash, and sterilize. We had purchased a handy travel microwaveable bottle steamer that worked well and was a convenient size for our small kitchen.

Before returning to work, I realized the need to set up a good routine for going to bed, waking up, and getting ready for work. Because of the time I needed to get up, Tamina and I went to bed at the same time, which made settling her to sleep quite easy, as she would feed on me until she fell asleep. As she wanted feeding, I would just give her my breast, hardly waking myself up. I allowed myself about two hours to get ready for work. This meant I could prepare food for the day, have breakfast, get dressed, and have time to ensure my baby had a good feed before I left.

I ensured the food I ate was healthy and provided me with the necessary energy to sustain a steady work-life schedule. What I did notice in my life was that I lacked "me" time. I felt my days were filled with work, baby, and husband. It was important to me to take some time out, so I started taking fifteen minutes in the morning to do some tapping, using the Emotional Freedom Technique (EFT), to relax my body and clear my mind. This step in my life was important and necessary to keep me focused and happy.

Work continued, and, thankfully, in my line of work, I get a good spread of holidays throughout the year, meaning I got to spend a lot of quality time with my family—the most important part of my life.

The Facts

Personal Time

With the birth of a baby and taking care of all his needs, it is easy to forget the importance of looking after yourself. However, to help you enjoy your life and time with your family, it is important, if not vital, to put time aside for yourself. By taking even fifteen minutes a day to partake in an activity you enjoy, such as reading, writing, meditating, tapping, or massage, you can experience more fulfillment in your life and revive your energies.

Tapping, commonly known as the Emotional Freedom Technique (EFT), is a method used to tap into your body's own energy and healing power by stimulating meridian points with your fingertips, combining Chinese acupuncture and modern psychology. It can be used for many circumstances in your life, such as, pain relief, stress relief, healing childhood traumas, body image, and many other areas (What is EFT Tapping? The Tapping Solution, 2013). For more information and some help with getting started, there are a number of useful Web sites and videos available.

Equipment Essentials

- Nappies (diapers) and baby wipes (unless using the "Elimination Communication" method)
- Padded changing mat (Mothercare has a good range)
- Clean blankets, clothes, and towels
- Baby bath (if you do not have a bath), sponge, head-to-toe body wash (Johnson's is a good brand, and it comes in an easy-to-use squirt bottle)
- Car seat (or a safe travelling carrier)
- Baby carrier (Baby Bjorn and Ergobaby make quality products)
- Sterilizer (travel microwaveable sterilizer is available from Mothercare)
- Hand pump (useful for when your breasts are full but your baby is not hungry).
- Baby bottles (BPA free)
- Cool bag and ice packs: If you plan on carrying breast milk in bottles, then this is needed especially in hot countries.
- Body thermometer
- Nasal aspirator (a simple device where you can suck out any blockages)
- For Mommy: Sanitary pads (big and high

absorbency), nursing bra (luxury), breast pads (you will leak!), accessible clothes for feeding.

Equipment Luxuries

- Electronic breast pump (There are a range available in shops and on Web sites.)
- Juicer and blender (to create healthy foods and drinks for you and, eventually, your baby)
- Pushchair/stroller: This can depend on your travelling needs. If you use taxis, you may want a compact and lightweight one that is easy to carry around.
- Stimulating toys, books, and music: At your baby's early stage, he or she will love black-and-white patterns.
- Cot (or basket): If you do not want your baby sleeping with you, then this is essential. If your baby sleeps in bed with you, it can be used as a barrier to stop your baby from rolling off the bed.
- Bouncing cradles and baby rockers
- Baby bag: You can use any bag you find comfortable to carry around.
- C-pillow
- Dummy/pacifier
- Teether

Documentation

When you are registering your baby for his or her birth certificate and passport, it is important that you provide the necessary documentation of both parents. This is likely to include

- birth certificates – If not in English, you must get them translated with certification (two copies). UK birth certificates must be the full A4 version, which can be obtained from: http://www.gro.gov.uk/gro/content/certificates/order_completion.asp;
- a copy of your marriage certificate;
- parents' passports;
- any other relevant identification documents, such as a Naturalization certificate or ID card; and
- baby photo.

For a British passport, go to the following website for more details: https://www.gov.uk/overseas-passports

Final Word

Parenthood is a blessing that comes with many responsibilities and challenges. When we enter into motherhood, many changes take place, some that we can prepare for and others that seem to take us by surprise. From my experience it really got me into gear, physically and mentally. I became more excited for my future, as my reason for living became more meaningful. I started taking time to reflect on my life, which led me to find a new energy that seemed to be hiding deep within me, one full of confidence, drive and ambition. Since having my baby I now feel more alive than ever and this inspired me to write this book so that I could positively pass on my joys and experiences to you. Through sharing my story and the related facts with you, it is my desire that you got a sense of what responsibilities and challenges you might face on your journey to motherhood and for it to have given you increased confidence and enjoyment.

Enjoy pregnancy, enjoy parenthood and most of all enjoy life. All will have a tremendous impact on your child.

Thank you for reading and have a happy and fulfilling parenthood!

Appendix A: Birthing plan example

<u>Sample Birth Plan</u>

1. Position—In labor: free to walk around. Birth: sitting up or on knees.
2. Support person: Husband
3. Amniotomy: I would prefer not to have my water broken artificially.
4. Natural birth: No pain relief unless I say.
5. Episiotomy: I would prefer to tear naturally rather than be cut.
6. Vaccine: Negative blood
7. Baby: I want to be given my baby as soon as she is born (or to her father).
8. Breast-feed baby immediately after birth. *No* formula to be given at any time.

If a C-section needs to be done (e.g., pregnancy diabetes, placenta preeclampsia, or baby in breech position at time of full term), I want to be awake

To pediatrician,
I want my baby to be breast-fed immediately. No formula must be given. I would like my husband to be with my baby when she is tested.

Appendix B: Things you might want to ask your doctor about

1. How much is the Thai Natural Birth Package going to cost (all going well)?
2. What does it include?
   - Three days, two nights: recovery room
   - Natural birth
     - o Petripon: Can I choose not to have any pain relief?
     - o Gas and air
     - o Epidural
     - o Fetal scalp monitor
     - o Episiotomy/stitching
     - o IV drip: If so, what is in it? Can I opt out of having it?
   - Labor/delivery room
   - Tearing: Will being stitched up be included in the cost?
   - What aftercare is given for tearing? Is iodine given for cleaning when peeing?
   - Cost of medical equipment used in delivery
   - In-utero electronic fetal heart rate monitoring
   - Operative obstetrics: forceps extraction, vacuum extraction
   - Rh-negative vaccine: Do they test baby's blood from cord tissue?
   - Nursing fee

- In-patient hospital service charge
- Daily meals: Any special requirements?
- Training: bathing baby, breast-feeding (lactation nurse team)
- Milk bottle
- Breast pump
- Diapers: how many?
- Maternity pants: how many?
- Blanket
- Newborn blood test
- Newborn vaccines: Eye antibiotic (teramicin ointment), Hep B, BCG, Vitamin K injection
- Hearing test for newborn (OAE)
- Obstetrician
- Pediatrician

3. If needed, how much would a Thai C-section cost?
4. Can I choose the position I give birth in?
5. Can I walk around during the first stage of labor?
6. I do not want to be coached. Can I push when my body needs to push?
7. Will my baby be given straight to me (or my husband) when born? For how long?
8. Can I breast-feed with in the first two hours?
9. I *do not* want my baby having *any* formula. How do I make sure this does not happen?
10. Can the baby's tests be performed with the mother and father present?
11. Do we get a baby photo?
12. Do you take footprints?

References, further reading, and useful videos and music

References

Books

Graham, Dr. Douglas N. *The 80/10/10 Diet: Balancing Your Health, Your Weight, and Your Life, One Luscious Bite at a Time.* Decatur: FoodnSport Press, 2006. Print.

Kindersley, Dorling, Dr. Carol Cooper, Harriet Griffey. *Johnson's Mother & Baby.* Great Britain: Dorling Kindersley, 2003. Print.

Articles

Bingo, Kru (2013) 'Thai phrases to keep unhealthy food away', *Expat Ladies in Bangkok*, October/November, pp. 61.

Web Sites

BabyCentre. "Having a Healthy Diet in Pregnancy." Accessed January 17, 2014. http://www.nhs.uk/conditions/pregnancy-and-baby/pages/healthy-pregnancy-diet.aspx#close.

BabyCentre. "Hernias." Accessed April 6, 2014. http://www.babycentre.co.uk/a551932/hernias.

BabyCentre. "Signs of Labour." Accessed March 27, 2014. http://www.babycentre.co.uk/signs-for-how-I-will-know-I-am-in-labour#ixzz2yHdARlWx.

BabyCentre. "The Top 10 Signs of Pregnancy." Accessed February 19, 2014. http://www.babycentre.co.uk/top-10-signs-of-pregnancy#ixzz2vYMAVayG.

Beier, Catherine. "Giving Birth Naturally, Routine Newborn Baby Care Procedures." Accessed April 6, 2014. http://www.givingbirthnaturally.com/newborn-baby-care.html.

KidsHealth. "Jaundice in Newborns." Accessed April 6, 2014. http://kidshealth.org/parent/pregnancy_center/newborn_care/jaundice.html.

Mumsnet By Parents for Parents. "Rhesus Negative and the Anti-D Injection." Accessed February 2, 2014. http://www.mumsnet.com/pregnancy/rhesus-negative-and-the-anti-d-injection.

NHS, "Epidural Anaesthesia." Accessed April 6, 2014. http://www.nhs.uk/conditions/Epidural-anaesthesia/Pages/Introduction.aspx.

NHS. "Fish and Shellfish." Accessed January 17, 2014. http://www.nhs.uk/Livewell/Goodfood/Pages/fish-shellfish.aspx.

The Tapping Solution. "What is EFT Tapping?" Accessed May 2, 2014. http://www.thetappingsolution.com/#what-is-eft-tapping.

Wikipedia: The Free Encyclopedia. "Mongolian Spot." Accessed April 6, 2014. http://en.wikipedia.org/wiki/Mongolian_spot.

Further Reading

A New Mum's Special Gift by Catherine Butcher

Babycentre: www.babycentre.co.uk

Baby Greens by Michaela Lynn and Michael Chrisemer, N. C.

Baby-led Weaning: Helping your baby to love good food by Gill Rapley & Tracey Murkett

Creating Healthy Children by Karen Ranzi

Johnson's Mother & Baby by DK

The 80/10/10 Diet by Douglas Graham, Dr.

The Tapping Solution: http://www.thetappingsolution.com/

Whole Baby Foods: www.wholebabyfoods.com

Useful Videos and Music

Awkward Hamster: http://www.youtube.com/user/AwkwardHamster (Videos that are particularly useful for fathers-to-be)

Baby Einstein (A series of programs with stimulating music and visuals)